MiM Mini Guide No.3: Speculative Suburban Houses 1928-38

Published in the United Kingdom 2022 by Mod in Metro Publishing

www.modernism-in-metroland.co.uk

Words, Photographs and Design by Joshua Abbott

Printed by Mixam Ltd, Watford

Joshua Abbott is hereby identified as the author of this work in accordance with Section 77 of the Copyrights, Designs and Patents Acts 1988.

A CIP Catalogue record is available for this book from the British Library.

All rights reserved. No part of this publication may be reproduced, stored in a retrieval system or transmitted in any form or by any means, electronic, mechanical, photocopying, recording or otherwise, without prior permission of the publishers.

ISBN: 978-1-7396857-2-0

MiM Mini Guide No.3:

Speculative Suburban Houses 1928-38

Joshua Abbott

"The House of Tomorrow that you live in Today"
Haymills Ltd Barn Hill Estate Advert 1932

Between the end of the First World War in 1918 and the beginning of the Second in 1939, an enormous housing boom took place around London and its neighbouring counties. Over 4 million new homes were built, partly fueled by David Lloyd George's "Homes fit for Heroes" pledge, an attempt to improve housing standard for the returning servicemen of World War I (and head off the threat of Bolshevism) and partly by the extension of various railways lines at the start of the 20th Century. The Metropolitan Railway had been the instigator of this speculative boom before 1914, using land left over from extending their lines to build estates marketed as "Metro-Land". The architecture of these new houses was a mixture of historical styles, taking elements from Tudor and Elizabethan eras and adding modern comforts inside.

One of the best examples of this balance between tradition and modernity was the Olympia House, a domestic design debuted at the 1935 Daily Mail Ideal Home exhibition by the John Laing building company, and later installed outside Kings Cross station. The house was built in brick with a pitched roof, but did feature curved metal windows and some models had a circular staircase tower. Examples of this house can be found in Edgware, Purley and elsewhere.

Modernism arose in the early part of the 20th Century, stripping decoration and elaboration in favour of simplicity and functionality. This style wasn't something that was taken up enthusiastically in Britain, with what later became known as Art Deco, contemporarily as Style or Jazz Moderne, accepted more readily. It came to fruition at the 1925 *Exposition internationale des arts décoratifs et industriels modernes* held in Paris, featuring pavilions from 20 countries. The curves and colours of deco found its home in cinemas, hotels and shops. A watered down version, often called 'streamline moderne', was used for speculative housing. These houses featured rendered white walls, curved windows and decorative details like sunrise motifs and chevrons.

This style of house became known as *"Suntrap"* due to the curved metal windows, and the practice that popularised it was Welch, Cachemaille-Day & Lander. The partnership was made up of three quite different architects; Herbert Welch, Felix Lander and Nugent Francis Cachemaille-Day. Welch was the eldest, a designer of many houses in Hampstead Garden Suburb from 1908 alongside Raymond Unwin. Lander also worked with Unwin, at Letchworth Garden City before moving to Welwyn Garden City where he met Cachemaille-Day. Cachemaille-Day would later be known as one of the finest church designers of the first half of the 20th century, and it is unclear how much hand he had in designing the partnership's housing estates.

The three designers went into practice together in 1930, with one of their first commissions being a small estate in Edgware for the developer Roger Malcolm, in Old Rectory Gardens. These houses represent one of the first meeting points between cosy English domestic and Continental modernity. Tiled, pitched roofs sit above white rendered walls, with curved metal windows. The partnership then produced a series of small speculative estates for Haymills Ltd of Golders Green. Estates were built at Hendon, Wembley and Hanger Hill, all featuring a mixture of traditional, modern and hybrid house designs. The suntrap spread its rays around suburbia with other building companies using the design to fit in with the streamlined spirit of the times. As Haymills adverts proclaimed *"Haymills capture the Modern Spirit. Great Advance in house design. Flat roof, soft grey facing bricks"*.

Welch, Cachemaille-Day & Lander also designed some suntrap houses for Hampstead Garden Suburb in the 1930s. The Suburb, founded by Henrietta Barnett and planned by Parker & Unwin and Edwin Lutyens from 1907, had generally been built in the prevailing Arts & Crafts and Neo-Georgian styles. However, outbreaks of modernism took place from the early 1930s. As well as the Welch, Cachemaille-Day & Lander houses, there are speculative moderne groups by C.M. Crickmer, Evelyn Simmons, G.G. Winbourne and others. Indeed Winbourne's Lytton Close from 1935 is one of the best groups of Art Deco houses in the capital.

Further out, the ancient country estates that encircled the capital began to be broken up at the start of the 20th century, with the upkeep costs too much for the younger inheritors of the prestigious houses. The Warren Estate in Stanmore, founded by the Duke of Chandos, was inherited by Sir John Fitzgerald in 1922. He decided to sell off parcels of land for development with two sets of houses being built along Valencia Road and Kerry Avenue by Douglas Wood Architects and Gerald Lacoste respectively.

Most suburban developments were driven by developers, and in some cases the developers forwent the need for outside architects all together. The fruits of those acting as both designers and developers (a practice that was previously banned) can be found all around the suburbs of London. Abbotshall Avenue in Enfield (Frank & Charles Woodward), Northwood Way in Hillingdon (Morgan & Edwards) and The Drive, Bexley (DC Bowyer & Sons) all showcase the mixture of modernity and commerce that powered the mid-1930s house building boom.

Some speculative developments were commissioned from the more famous modernist designers. The partnership of Connell, Ward & Lucas designed two groups of rigorous white walled houses at Amersham and Ruislip. The four Sun Houses at Amersham were built just below High and Over, the pioneering modernist houses designed by Amyas Connell in 1929 for archaeologist and art historian Prof Bernard Ashmole. They also designed another four houses for what was supposed to be an estate of Bauhaus-influenced dwellings in leafy Ruislip. The public were not as taken with these futuristic designs as the developers and architects, and no more were built.

Other famous architects designing speculative houses in the suburbs include Berthold Lubetkin, who alongside A.V. Pilichowski produced a bold terrace of four houses in Plumstead. Ernst Freud, son of Sigmund, designed a group of six houses in Hampstead with attached garages. Wells Coates, designer of the streamlined Isokon flats in Belsize Park, developed his Sunspan house with David Pleydell-Bouverie, initially for the Daily Mail 1934 Ideal Home exhibition. Groups of Sunspan houses can still be found in New Malden and Surrey.

The 1934 Ideal Home exhibition at Olympia in Kensington was perhaps the high water mark for modernist influenced suburban housing. Its 'Village of Tomorrow' comprised a number of moderne houses from various building firms. Morrells, Wates, E & L Berg, Davis Estates and others showcased flat roofed, white walled house designs that they hoped would appeal to the mass market. Of course, this wasn't to be and at the next year's exhibition only one overtly modernist house was exhibited, with others showing select elements of the new style rather than the whole package.

The exhibition estate was a ploy also used by developers to try and sell the idea of modernist living to reluctant home buyers in the 1930s. The 1934 Modern Homes Exhibition at Gidea Park in Havering, was a retread of an exhibition held in 1911 to showcase Arts & Crafts houses. Around 35 modernist derived houses were built for the 1934 exhibition, with many now having been extended and altered. The most uncompromisingly modernist of the lot was the cubist 64 Heath Drive by Francis Skinner of Lubetkin's Tecton group, now Grade II listed.

Much further east is the Frinton Park Estate, an attempt to make a modernist estate by the sea, overseen by Oliver Hill. Buyers were supposed to purchase a plot of land and engage an architect from the estates list to design a new house, The list was a who's who of 1930s modernist architects in Britain; Erich Mendlesohn, Serge Chermayeff, Maxwell Fry, Wells Coates, F.R.S. Yorke and Connell, Ward & Lucas among them. That plan failed, so in the end around 25 show homes were built for the prospective modernist home buyer, most of which survive (see Mini Guide No.1).

Since the 1930s, many of the houses built in the speculative suburban boom have succumbed to demolition, deterioration and redesign. Flat roofs have been replaced with pitched, white render by tile hanging, roof terraces with extra bedrooms and front gardens with driveways. A few have been listed, such as Kemp and Taskers work for Morrells in Herne Hill and Bromley, but much has now been lost or disfigured.

This mini guide is an attempt to map the record houses and document their design and history. The houses in the guide are arranged in roughly geographical order, starting in the north and travelling clockwise around the capital's suburbs. Each entry includes the street name, build date, architect's name (if known) and developers (if known). There is also a small portion of text giving information about the design and history of the houses. Also included are a variety of houses without a build date or architect's name but which represent the stylistic diversity of the modernist speculative suburban house.

Old Rectory Gardens, Edgware
Barnet
1928-32
Welch, Cachemaille-Day & Lander
Roger Malcolm

One of the first examples of the modernist speculative house in the suburbs of London and in Britain, was built at the end of the Northern Line in Edgware. The Portsdown estate comprised five acres, facing the underground station, which had opened in 1923. It was developed by the firm of Roger Malcolm, with a cinema, shops and 26 houses on what became Old Rectory Gardens. They were designed by Herbert Welch of Welch, Cachemaille-Day & Lander, instigator of the Suntrap style, a compromise between moderne stylings and traditional house forms. In the current day, the houses are mostly intact, although only one house still has metal windows and a number of the lovely deco doorways have been replaced with porches.

Elsewhere in Edgware are a number of other suntrap estates; Mill Ridge (1934), another Malcolm development, with a prominent detached house on the corner, Mowbray Road, featuring a group of green pantiled houses, and Highview Avenue, with three detached houses showcasing their original decoration. The streets to the north, across Edgware Way, feature the more common speculative house of the era; crescents of brick and tile homes by developers and builders John Laing Ltd.

87-91 Highview Avenue

Mill Ridge

29-46 Ashley Lane & 47 Sherwood Road, Hendon
Barnet
1933
Welch, Cachemaille-Day & Lander
Haymills Ltd.

72 Downage, Hendon
Barnet
1936
Charles Evelyn Simmons
Haymills Ltd.

Like many of the villages around London, Hendon was slowly subsumed into the growing capital by the introduction of various transport networks. The railway arrived in 1868, followed by the underground and the Hendon Way road in the early 1920s. The grounds of the large country houses such as Hendon Hall were sold off with developers laying out various new housing estates. Haymills' Hancock Estate covered the area to the west of Hendon Hall, with a mixture of traditional and modernist detached houses. Welch, Cachemaille-Day & Lander designed a number of houses on *Ashley Lane* and *Sherwood Road* in a similar style to their designs at Barn Rise, Wembley; flat roofs with tiled parapets, unrendered brick and sun decks. Unfortunately only one still exists in an unaltered form, with most having been demolished.

There are some more spectacular designs on the estate than the Welch, Cachemaille-Day & Lander houses. *5 Ashley Lane*, by an unknown architect, features white rendered walls beneath a green pantiled roof, a staircase tower with vertical windows and a wonderful recessed doorway. One street over is *72 Downage*, designed by Charles Evelyn Simmons. The house was originally produced for the 1934 Ideal Home Exhibition, and named "The Sunway". It was aimed at the higher end of the speculative market, being detached from its neighbours and featuring a sunroof, balconies, tall staircase tower and integrated garage. Despite its glamour and sophistication, the Sunway design did not catch on with the public with only a handful built.

72 Downage

31 Ashley Lane

47 Sherwood Road

5 Ashley Lane

Claremont Park, Finchley

Marlborough Avenue, Arnos Grove

1-8 Lytton Close, Hampstead Garden Suburb
Barnet
1935
G.G. Winbourne
W.L.M. Estates

Planted amongst the overwhelmingly arts and crafts landscape of Hampstead Garden Suburb, are a number of speculative houses influenced by modernism and art deco. The most accomplished group are those in *Lytton Close*, built in 1935 and designed by G.G. Winbourne. The group comprises detached, semi-detached and terraced houses, all in bright white render. Decoration is minimal, but the exteriors feature curved windows, metal balconies and rooftop terraces.

Elsewhere in the suburb, Welch, Cachemaille-Day & Lander contributed two groups of their Suntrap houses at *Kingsley Close* and *Ossulton Way*. These houses stick to their previous speculative designs, featuring curved windows and tiled, overhanging roofs. Similar houses by C.M. Crickmer appear on *Hutchings Walk* and *Howard Walk*, with both detached and semi-detached designs, featuring garages decorated with wavy lines.

In *Vivian Way* are two groups of houses built with flat roofs, a rarity in the suburb. Nos.20 & 22 were designed by George B. Drury & Fraser Reekie, with curved frontages and strong horizontal window sills and parapets running around the roofline. Nos. 24-30 were designed by G. Brian Herbert, and when built, were strong modernist designs with ribbon windows and integrated garages. All four houses have now had tiled, pitched roofs added but they are still well preserved.

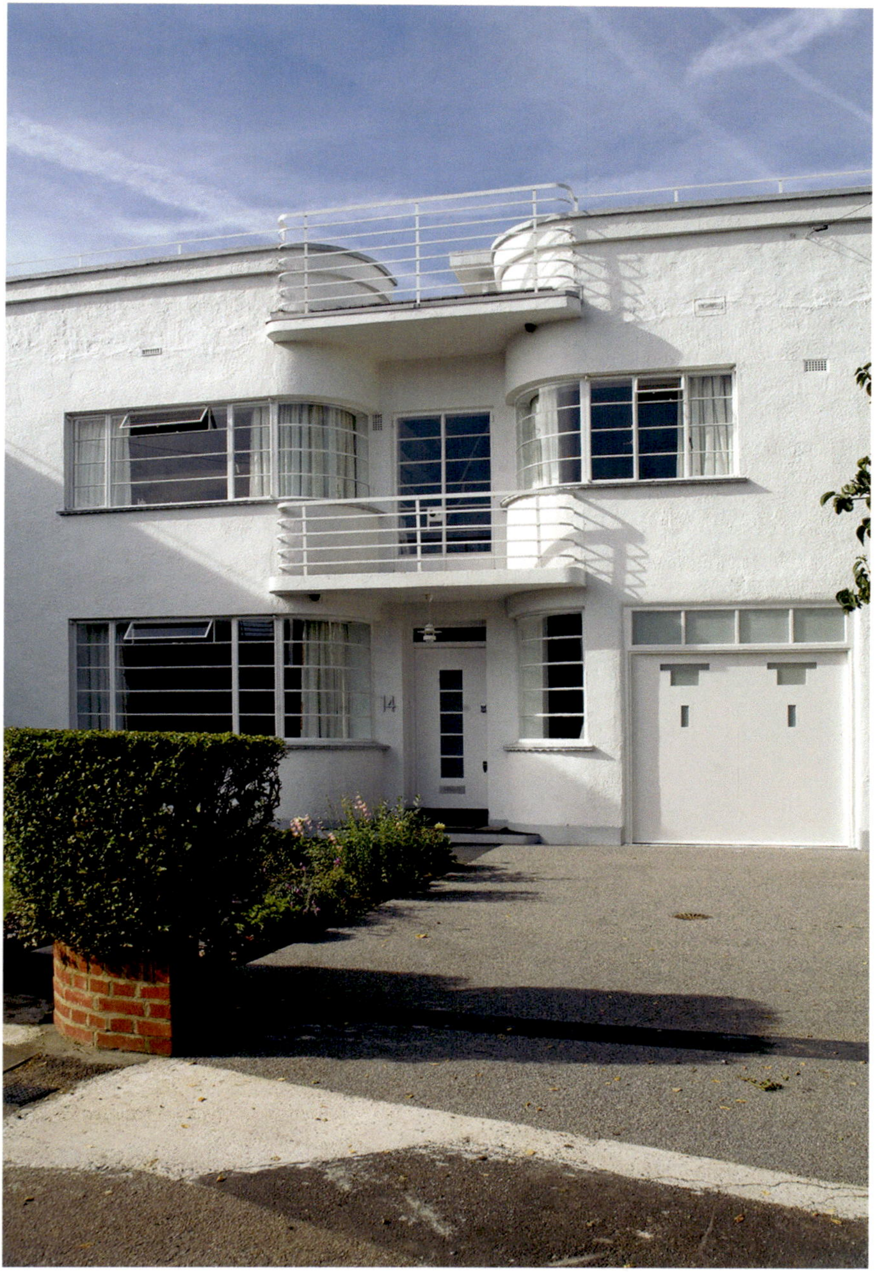
14

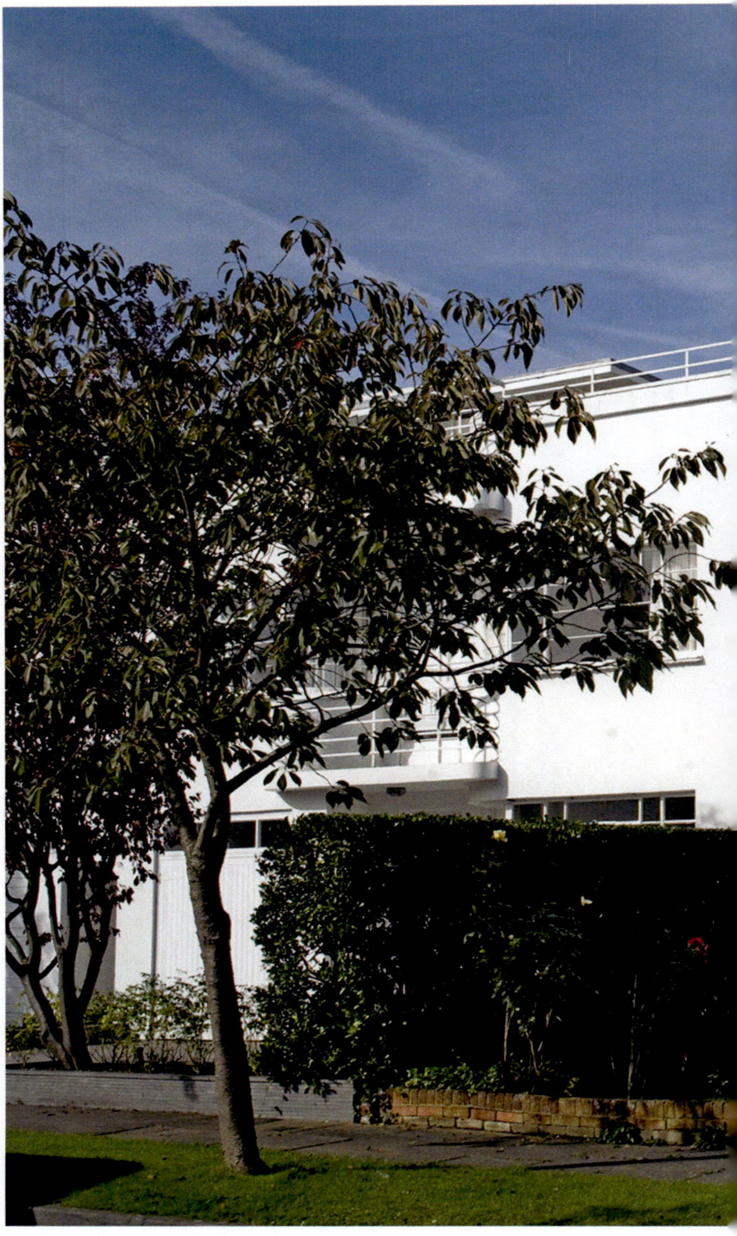

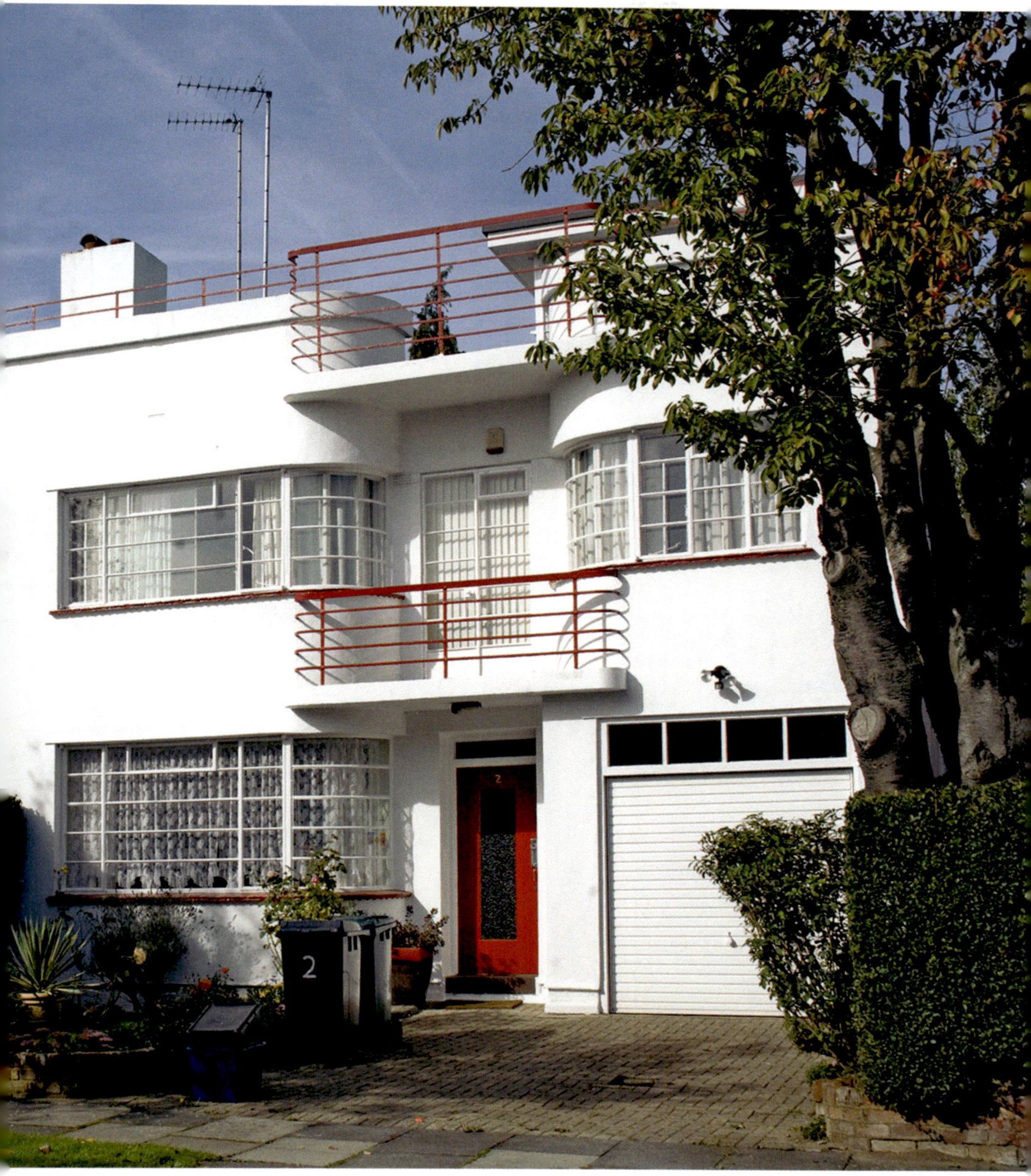
2

Kingsley Close

Vivian Way

Ossulton Way

1-17 Abbotshall Ave, Arnos Grove
Enfield
1935-7
Frank Woodward
Frank & Charles Woodward

On the slopes of North London, just beyond the north circular, lie this group of eight art deco speculative houses. They were built by developers Frank & Charles Woodward, and seemingly designed by Frank, who was also an architect. This conflict of interest had previously been prohibited in the 1920s, but was subsequently allowed to encourage small-scale building after the Great Depression. The houses are designed in the marketable "jazz modern" style of the era. The houses are a mix of detached and semi detached, with flat roofs and integrated garages. The houses have a great horizontal emphasis, with decorative stripes, suntrap windows and projecting ledges. The state of the houses today runs the gamut from well preserved to dilapidated.

A 10 minute walk away is *Whitehouse Way*, a similar collection of deco inspired houses, built by the developers Davis Estates Ltd in 1935. Like the Abbotshall Ave houses, they have a strong horizontal accent with curved windows and striped decoration. Unlike those houses, they have been somewhat altered, with a few now sporting pitched roofs. Davis built around 26 estates through suburban London in the interwar period, at Eltham, Petts Wood, Harrow and many other locations.

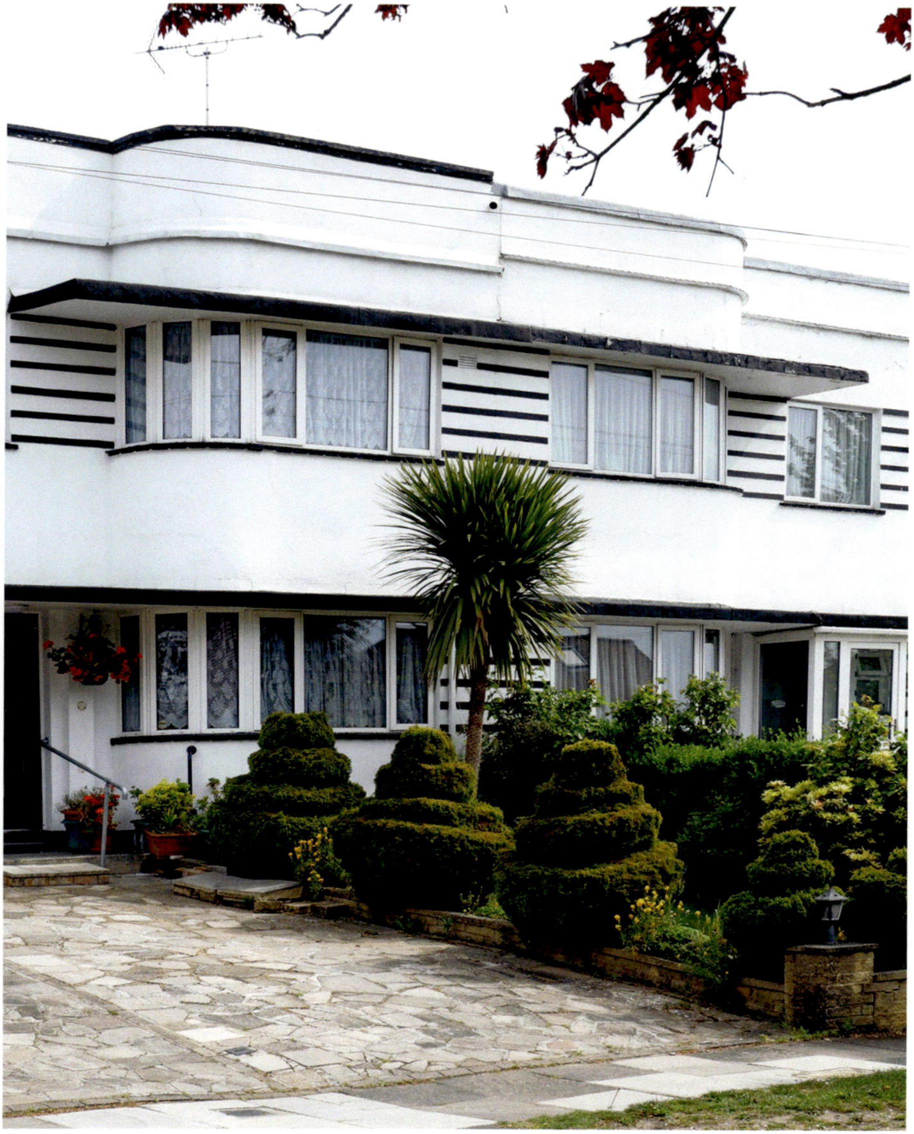

Abbotshall Avenue

Whitehouse Way

1-6 Frognal Close, Hampstead
Camden
1936
Ernst L. Freud
Ralph Davis

A group of six semi-detached houses in genteel Frognal area of Hampstead. They were designed by Ernst L. Freud, son of Sigmund, one of his largest commissions in the London-based part of his career. The houses are built in brick, not rendered as found elsewhere, and designed with garages and maids quarters. Rather more reticent than most modernist speculative houses, the grey brick Frognal Close dwellings are largely hidden by tall bushes. One detail that peeps above the greenery are the windows, with raised panels around some and porthole designs for others.

His other most notable design in London is the Belvedere Court apartments in Hampstead Garden Suburb, three connected blocks of flats built for Jewish families arriving from Europe, now listed like the Frognal Close houses. Most of Freud's later commissions would be conversions and interior works.

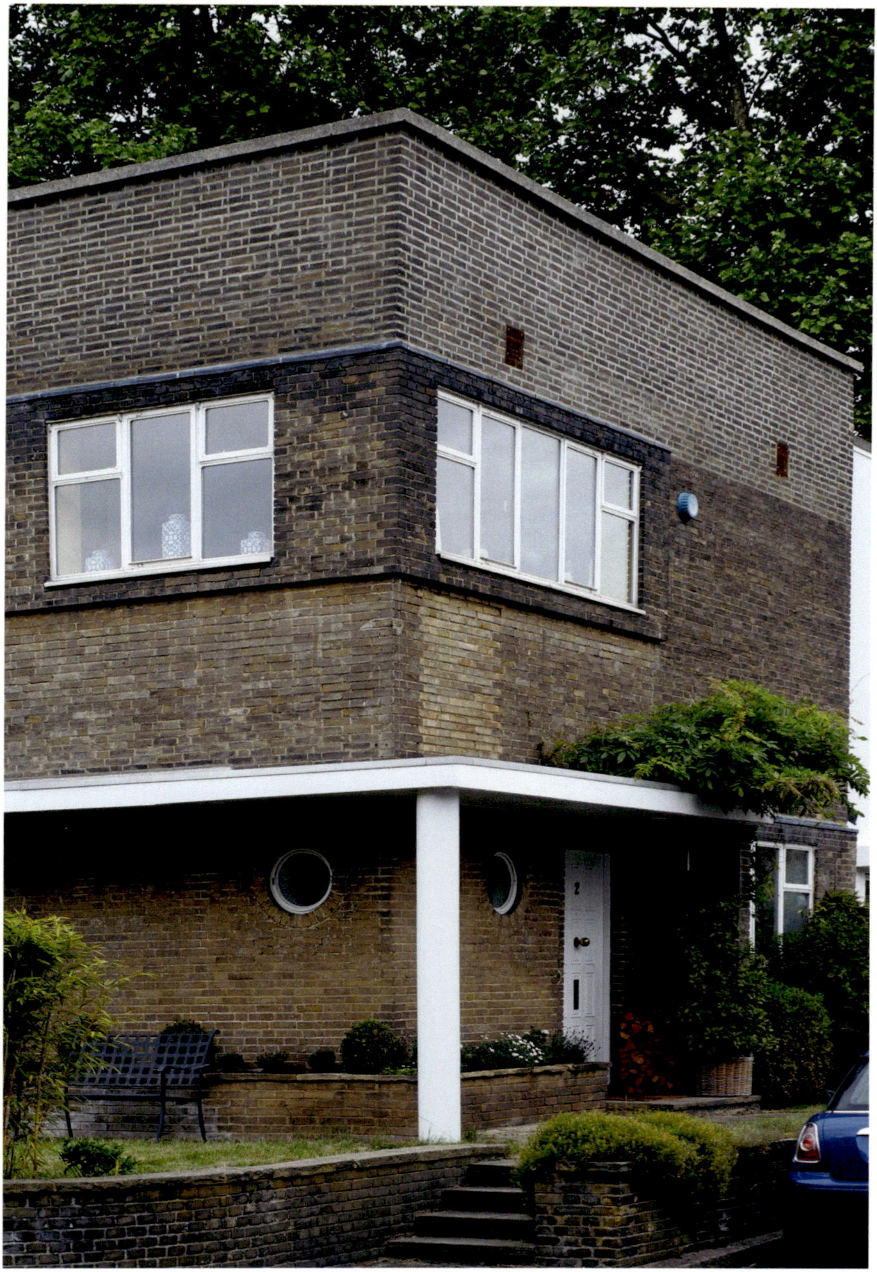
2

1 & 3 Willow Road, Hampstead
Camden
1938
Erno Goldfinger
Erno & Ursula Goldfinger

Elsewhere in Hampstead is the famous home of Erno Goldfinger. Built in 1938, No.2 was home to Goldfinger and his wife Ursula for nearly 60 years, and is now a National Trust property. Nos. 1 and 3 were built as speculative homes, with their sales helping to offset the construction costs. The three houses form a single terrace with the Goldfingers house in the centre. They are three storeys in height from the street, with an extra storey to the rear. The houses are constructed with a concrete frame and a red brick facing.

Each house is centred around a spiral staircase, engineered by Ove Arup and designed to maximise floor space. The design of the houses, in the middle of leafy Hampstead, caused a planning furore with many objectors complaining that the houses would be out of place with their historical neighbours. The plan was turned down by Hampstead Borough Council, but Goldfinger successfully argued that the design was in keeping with Georgian terraces and won an appeal with London County Council.

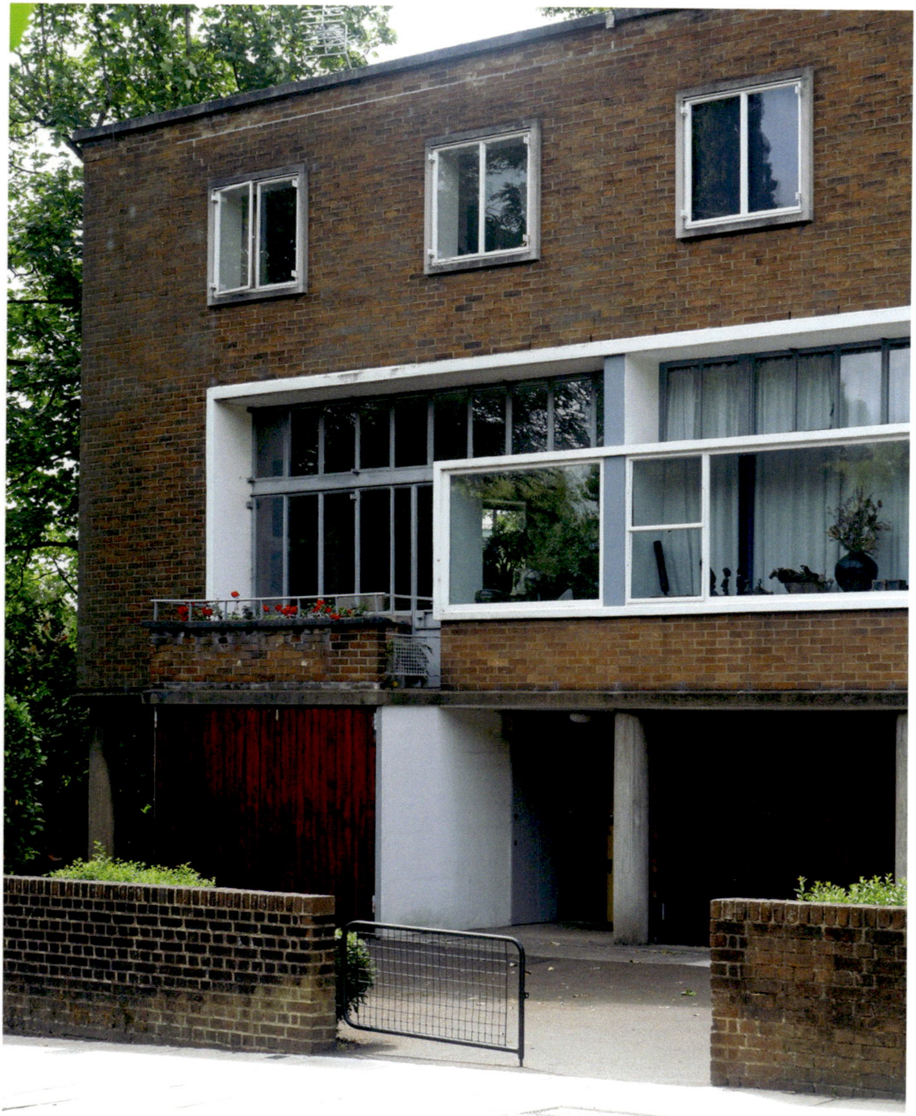

Gidea Park Exhibition Houses
Havering
1934
Various
Gidea Park Modern Homes Exhibition 1934

The 1911 Gidea Park Exhibition was held to showcase contemporary house design and town planning, with over 150 homes built, mainly in the dominant Arts and Crafts style. 23 years later a further 35 houses were built and exhibited in a "Modern Homes Exhibition". This time modernism was the style on show, with designs from architects such as Tecton and F.R.S. Yorke. The houses were sorted into different classes according to size, price and setting, with winners and runners up awarded in each category by a jury which included architects Maxwell Fry and Clifford Culpin.

64 Heath Drive, designed by Francis Skinner of Tecton, was the winner of Class E. With its L-shaped plan, sheer white concrete walls and minimal windows, it was by far the most modernist design of the exhibition. The house was planned with a large, flexibly arranged living area and a sun terrace leading off from the main bedroom. 64 Heath Drive was listed in 1997 and the interiors restored having been altered by a previous owner.

The other 1934 houses were not as stridently modernist as No.64. Its neighbour, No.62 designed by John Leech, took a more art deco approach with a recessed doorway and central window. Elsewhere, facing the ceaseless traffic of Eastern Avenue, are a pair of semi-detached concrete houses by F.R.S. Yorke, alongside W.G. Holford & G. Stephenson. One half has been altered, but the other (No.324) still sports the thin steel columns that support the projecting first floor. Altered is the state of much of the rest of the housing on the estate, proving the clamour for modernist housing has not increased much since 1934.

62 Heath Drive

320 & 322 Eastern Avenue East

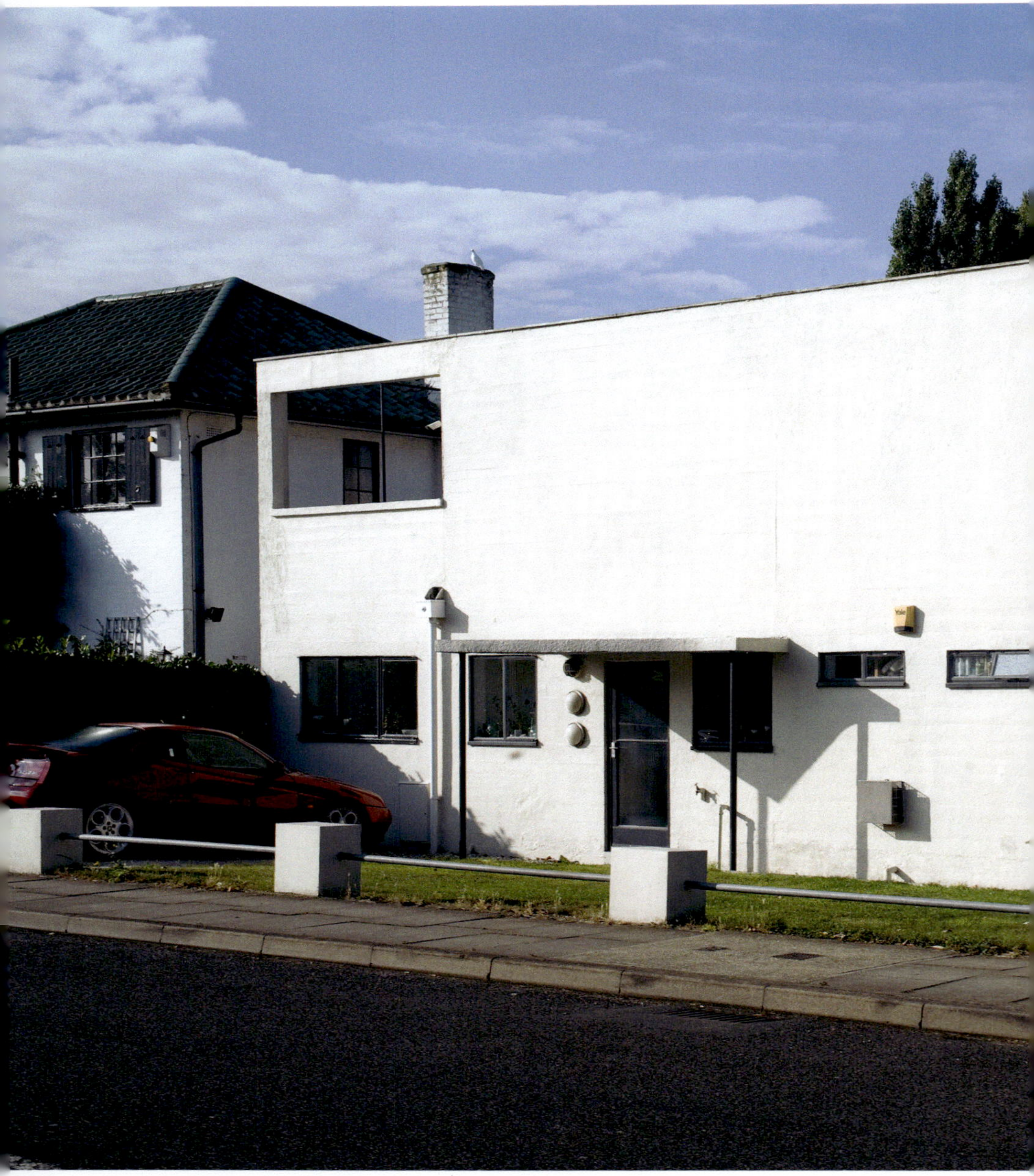

64 Heath Drive

85-91 Genesta Road, Plumstead
Greenwich
1934
Berthold Lubetkin & A.V. Pilichowski
CJ Pell & Co/George West Ltd.

One of the foremost modernist architects in Britain in the 1930s was Berthold Lubetkin. Born in Russia, Lubetkin arrived in Britain in 1931, after working in Paris. In London he set up the Tecton practice, finding fame with their designs for London Zoo and the Highpoint apartments at Highgate. Lubetkin's fellow emigre architect A.V. Pilichowski, secured a commission for a terrace of houses in Plumstead in 1933. Placed amid a typical street of Victorian houses, the four townhouses dazzle with their white rendered concrete walls, projecting windows and sculptural balconies, (Lubetkin would use the same balcony design at Highpoint).

The terrace is constructed in reinforced concrete, insulated with cork. The houses are three storeys in height with integrated garages on the ground floor, living areas on the first and bedrooms on the second. The rear of the houses face north with a view looking towards the River Thames. The houses are now Grade II* listed and kept in excellent condition. Lubetkin would design another speculative project this time with Tecton, in Haywards Heath, West Sussex. That scheme features eight brick houses with curved doorways and projecting ground floor balconies, and is now also listed.

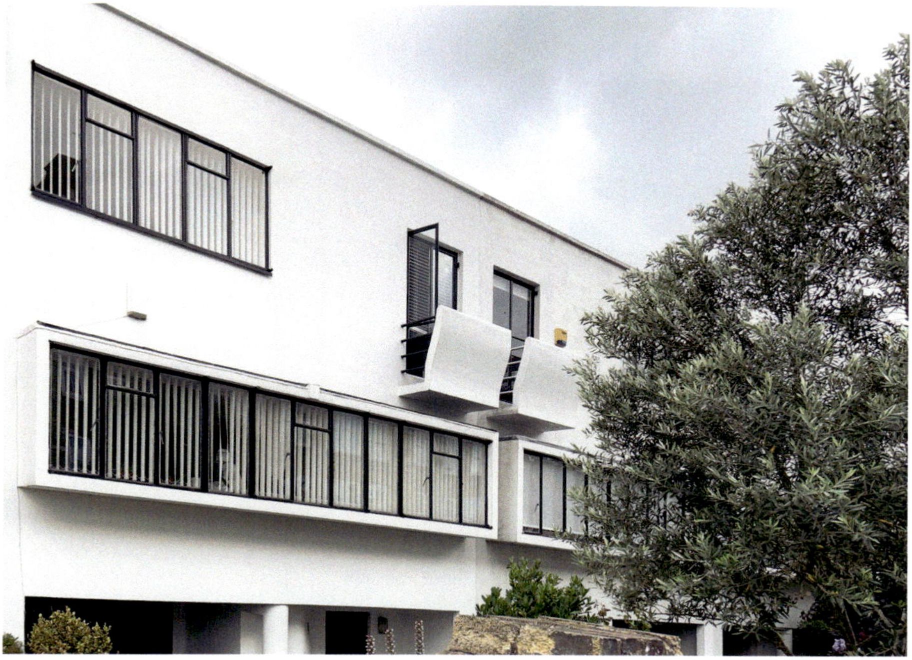

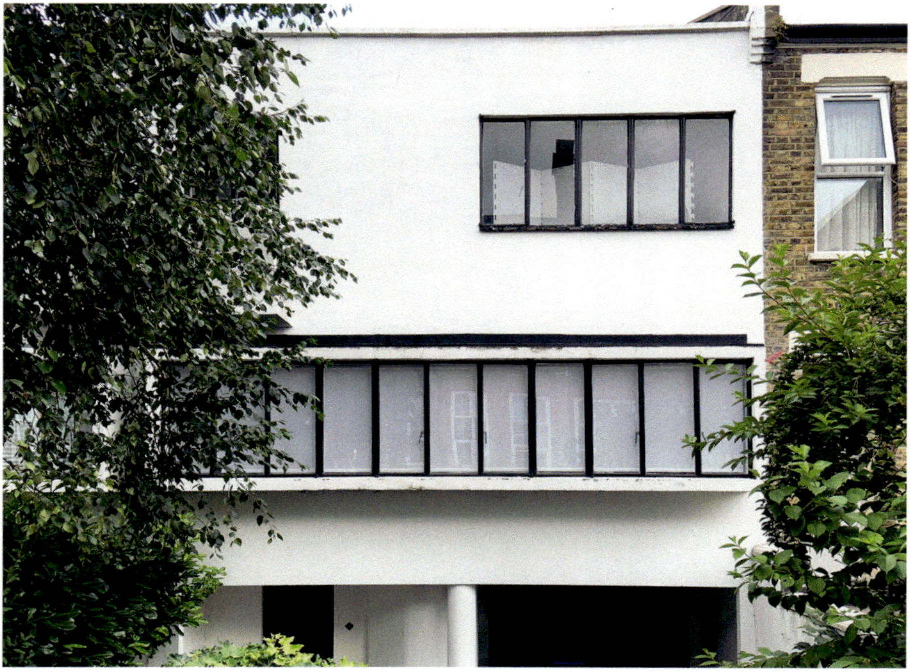

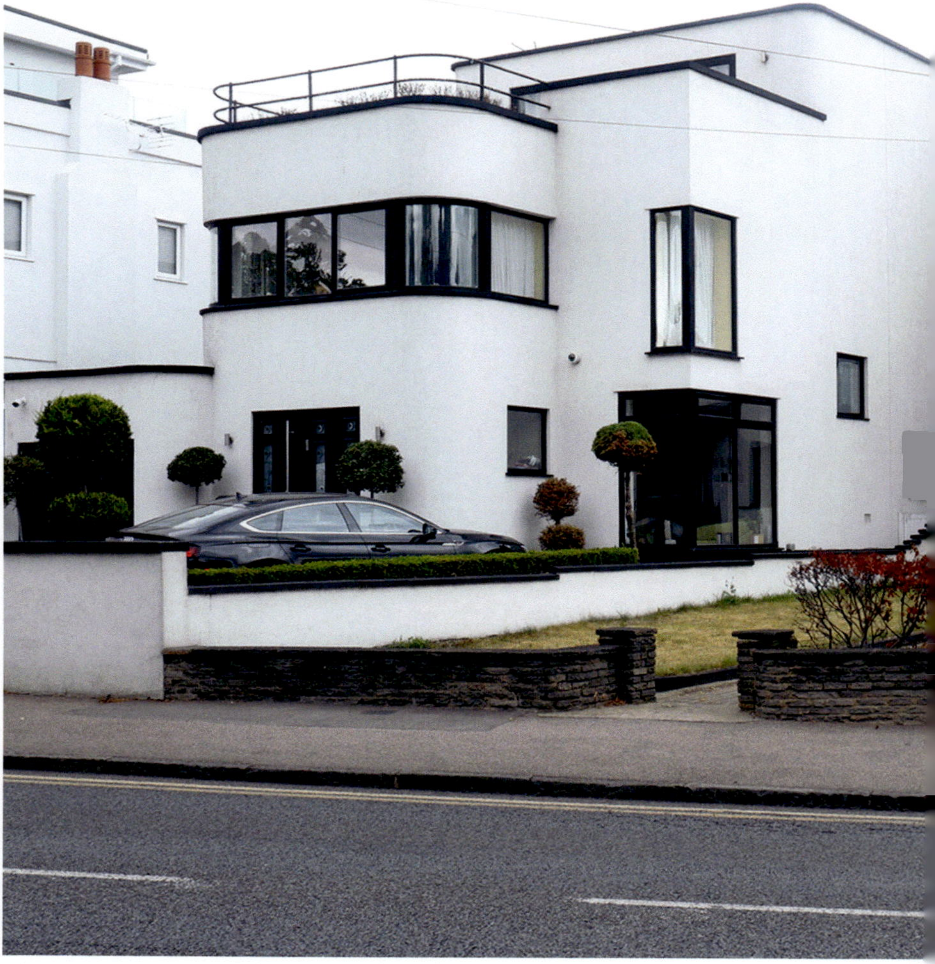

67-81 Danson Road, Bexleyheath
Bexley
1934
D.C. Wadhwa and Frederick Jones
Martin & Co.

A collection of eight houses of varying modernist influence, facing Danson Park in Bexleyheath. They were erected by the builders Martin & Co, who employed the architect D.C. Wadhwa to design ten houses in total. Wadhawa was born in Multan, in what is now Pakistan, and had come to Britain to practise with an office in Regent Street. Wadhwa designed Nos. 69-75 for the building firm, combining white rendered walls, sun decks and an interesting arrangement of windows. This seemingly proved too much for the locals, and another architect Frederick H. Jones was drafted in to design Nos. 77-81, which still boasted flat roofs and white walls but were not as daring as Wadhwa's designs. The houses have had some alterations and extensions including a couple of pitched roofs added, but they still project the spirit of 1930s in the 21st century.

93-99 The Drive
Bexley
1934
D.C. Bowyer & Sons Builders
Blendon Hall Estate

This area of Bexley had been the residence of the de Blaindon family from the 14th century, and the Georgian country villa Blendon Hall was built in 1763. The hall and its grounds were bought by a local builder, D.C. Bowyer, in 1929, and he started building speculative houses soon after. Most were in the traditional house style of the era, semi detached with half timbering and pitched roofs. However Bowyer built a few that bucked this trend. The best survivors are 93-99 The Drive, two pairs of semi detached moderne houses.

Nos. 97 and 99 have curved staircase towers and rooftop decks, with slightly unfortunate replacement windows and added porches. Nos. 93 and 95 are joined in a U-plan, with 93 having a mixture of render and exposed brick, as well as some jolly iron railings. Until recently No.95 had had a pitched roof and tile hanging installed. Now thankfully removed, the house has been made over to look like a pristine 1930s modernist build. There are a couple more houses on the surrounding streets that were moderne but now feature added roofs, extensions and 'improvements'.

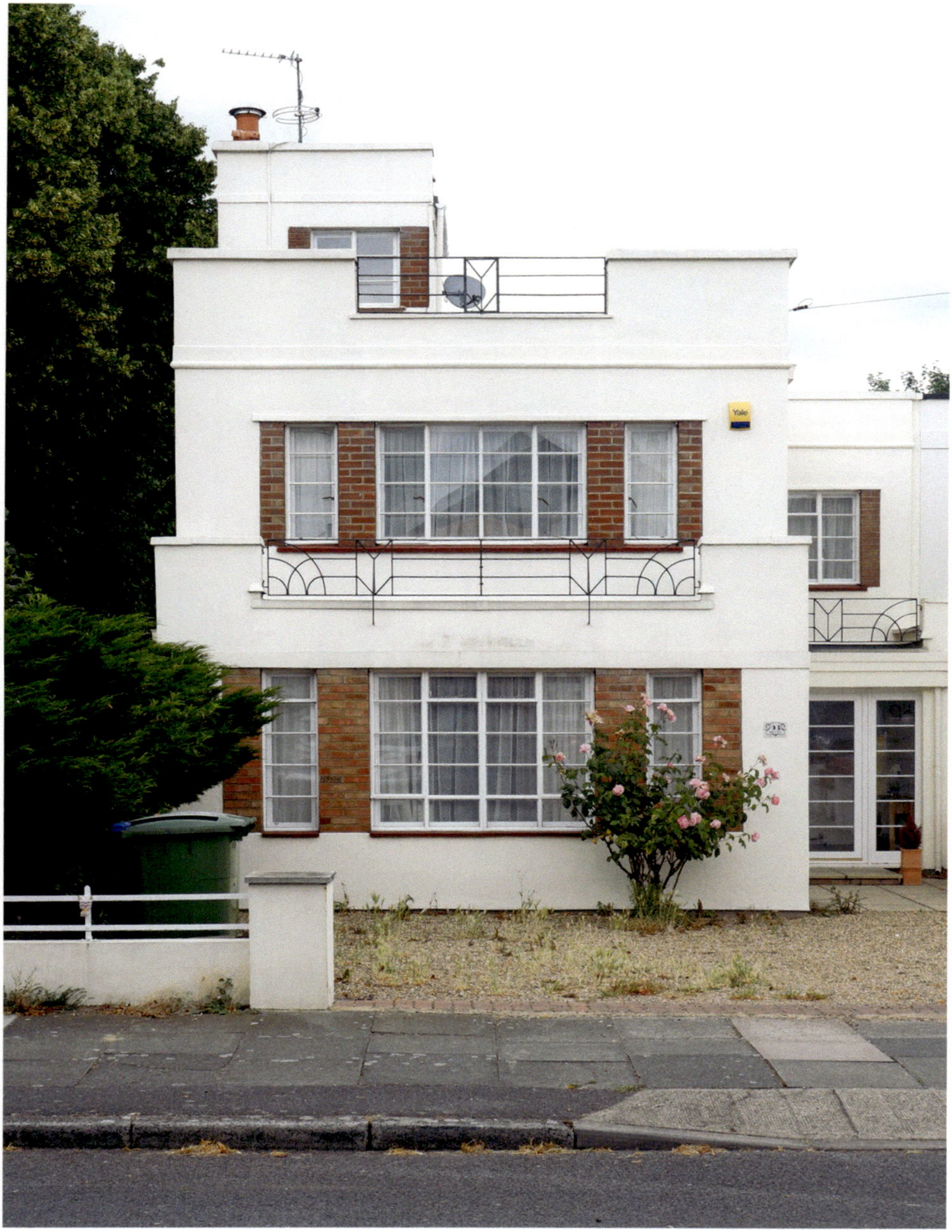
Yale

Hill Crescent, Coldblow
Bexley
1936
C.D. Dixon
H.L. Jeanes

Hill Crescent sits just outside Old Bexley, a circular street featuring a mix of detached modernist and traditional houses. It was developed by H.L. Jeanes in the mid-30s, after he had purchased the Ravenscourt estate and decided to build speculative houses on the land. The modernist influenced houses are at the start of the street, a mixture of art deco and streamline moderne designs. The best preserved houses are Nos. 2 and 7. No.2 sits at the entrance to the crescent, a perfect slice of Hollywood moderne with its curved windows, green pan tiled roof and geometric doorway. No.7 is more modernist in tone, featuring a rooftop sun deck, metal windows and curved frontage.

The other houses have been altered somewhat but still retain their modernist influences. The houses seem to have been designed by C.D. Dixon, and the more traditional ones by G.J. Robinson Claridge, both obscure figures. The plans for the estate hint that the designs were produced from drawings by Jeanes himself. This versatility doesn't seem to have proven a success with Jeanes being declared bankrupt in 1937 and again in 1950. This collection of houses remain as his legacy.

7 Hill Crescent

9 Hill Crescent

2 Hill Crescent

2 & 4 Mead Way, Hayes
Bromley
1934
E. Willson
H. Boot (Garden Estates) Ltd

On the corner of Mead Way and Hayes Lane, just south of Bromley, sit these two modernist houses in a sea of traditional looking semis. Both types of houses were built by H. Boot (Garden Estates) Ltd, a subsidiary of the builders Henry Boot & Sons. The new company had been set up to build an estate on land the company had purchased between Bromley and Hayes. The company built nearly 1000 houses in the area before concentrating on other opportunities.

The lone flat-roofed semi-detached pair were the only modernist influenced houses built, due to the local authorities reluctance to grant permission to any more. They were most probably designed by E. Willson, the architect who produced a number of other houses for Henry Boot. The company also put up some flat roofed terraced houses in Wickham Chase, not far from Mead Way. These houses are now altered with pitched roofs and added porches.

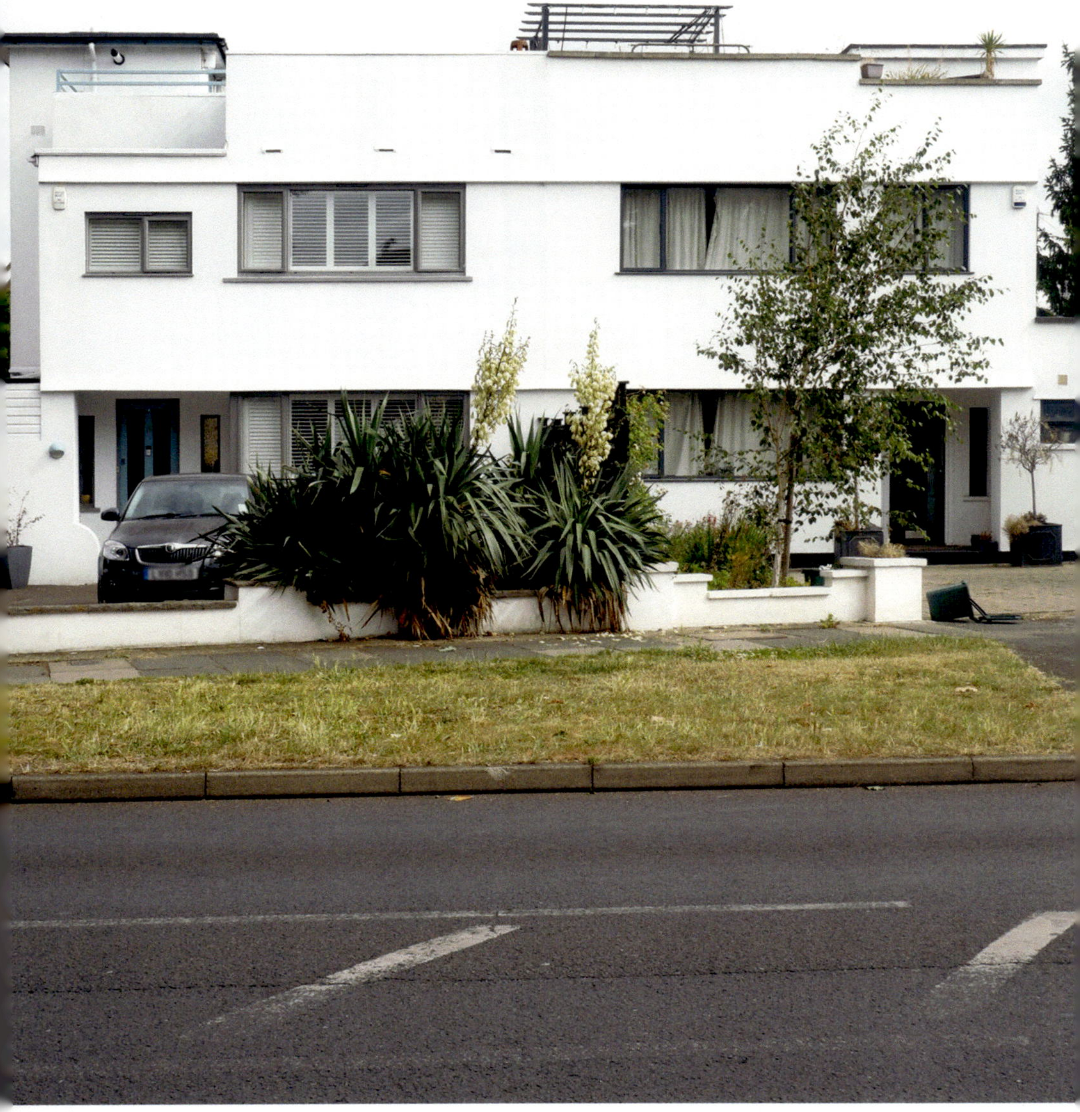

82-90 Bushey Way, Park Langley
Bromley
1935
Rogers Brothers
Health Ray Development Co

The Langley estate had been around for over 800 years, passing from storied family to family until the early 20th century when it was sold off for development. The main developer was H&G Taylor who created a garden suburb in the years before the First World War. Smaller estates were built after 1918, including this collection of art deco houses on Bushey Way. The designer of the houses is unknown, but they were built by the surveyors and builders Rogers Brothers on behalf of the Health Ray Development Company.

There are five flat roofed houses, detached apart from their conjoined garages. The houses are two storeys with a top floor sun deck. The exteriors feature original details such as the lozenge decoration on the parapet and the corner doorway. Next to these five are two houses with green pantiled pitched roofs and built in garages. Both sets of houses seem to be set in the same plan with a projecting frontage. The developers may have been hedging their bets and providing designs that were not quite as modern as their neighbours in the hopes of maximising sales.

86

Seaforth Gardens, Epsom

Elsiemaud Road, Ladywell

Dorchester Drive, Herne Hill
Lambeth
1935
Kemp & Tasker
Morrell Ltd

Twin brothers Cyril and Herbert Morrell were significant builders and developers in the southeast of London in the interwar period. Like other developers mentioned in this guide, the Morrells built estates largely in the Tudorbethan style with a few modernist influenced homes sprinkled here and there. They employed architects Leslie H. Kemp and Frederick E. Tasker, more widely known for their cinemas, to produce a house design for use on a number of sites. The pair debuted their design at ther 1934 Ideal Home Exhibition, with the selling point that it could be built in any part of the country and adapted to the clients needs. In the end only three were built, at Dorchester Drive in Herne Hill, at 77 Addington Road, West Wickham and another in Dublin that was seemingly copied from Kemp and Tasker's design.

The house at Dorchester Drive was built as part of a larger scheme from the Morrells. As well as the exhibition house at number 10, Kemp & Tasker designed the Tudorbethan *"Tudor Stacks"* (intended for the Morell's mother, now demolished), *"Dorchester House"* for the two brothers (now listed) and Dorchester Court, an apartment complex that is also listed but run down. The exhibition house has now been listed after nearly being demolished. It was home for many years to the psychologist Hans Eyseneck, and has had a few alterations, but retains itsflexible internal plan which allows for the ground floor to be opened up into a large entertainment space for parties and gatherings. The Morrells also built other, less distinct moderne houses on *Green Gates Road, West Wickham* by T. Spencer Bright before they were bankrupted by a mortgage payment strike at the Coney Hall estate.

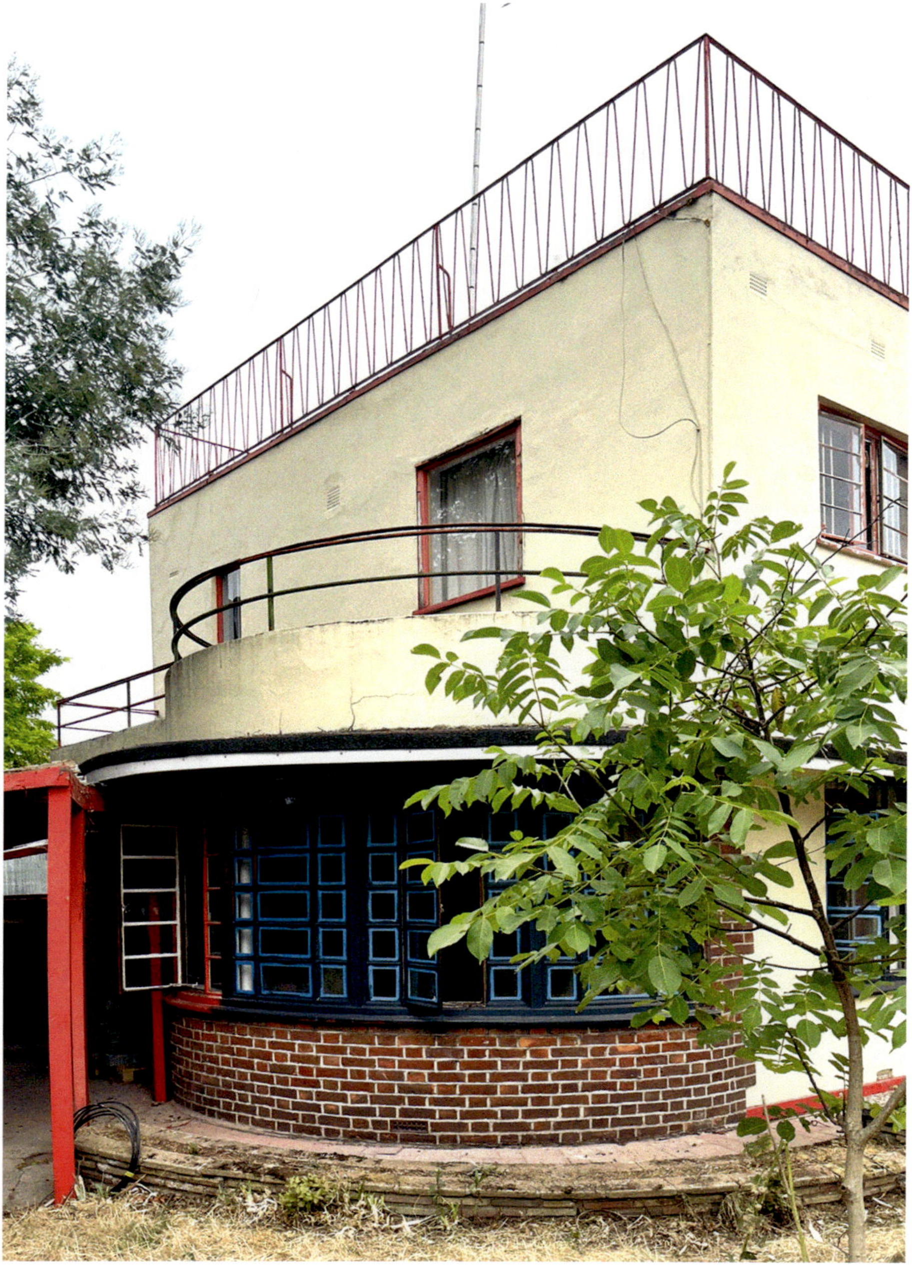

77 Addington Road, West Wickham

Gates Green Road, West Wickham

Elmbridge Avenue & Grand Avenue, Surbiton
Kingston upon Thames
1934
Bell Property Trust

Just north of the A3 in Surbiton is one of the bigger groups of flat roofed speculative houses in Greater London. They were built by the Bell Property Trust as part of the Berrylands Estate in 1934, with the houses situated in a wedge along the meeting point of Elmbridge Avenue and Grand Avenue. There are three different designs of houses, all with flat roofs but some houses have a central staircase tower whilst others have projecting frontages. All houses were built in brick with some left exposed and others rendered white.

The houses were advertised in the sales brochure as "Luxury Modern Residences at Moderate Prices..". The Bell Property Trust built a number of luxurious apartment blocks around London in the 1930s, including Ealing Village, built to house the stars of the nearby Ealing Studios and various apartment buildings in Streatham. These estates were designed by the firm of R. Toms & Partners, although it is not known whether they were involved in the Berrylands Estate. In the present day the houses are generally intact, albeit with the usual replacement UPVC windows

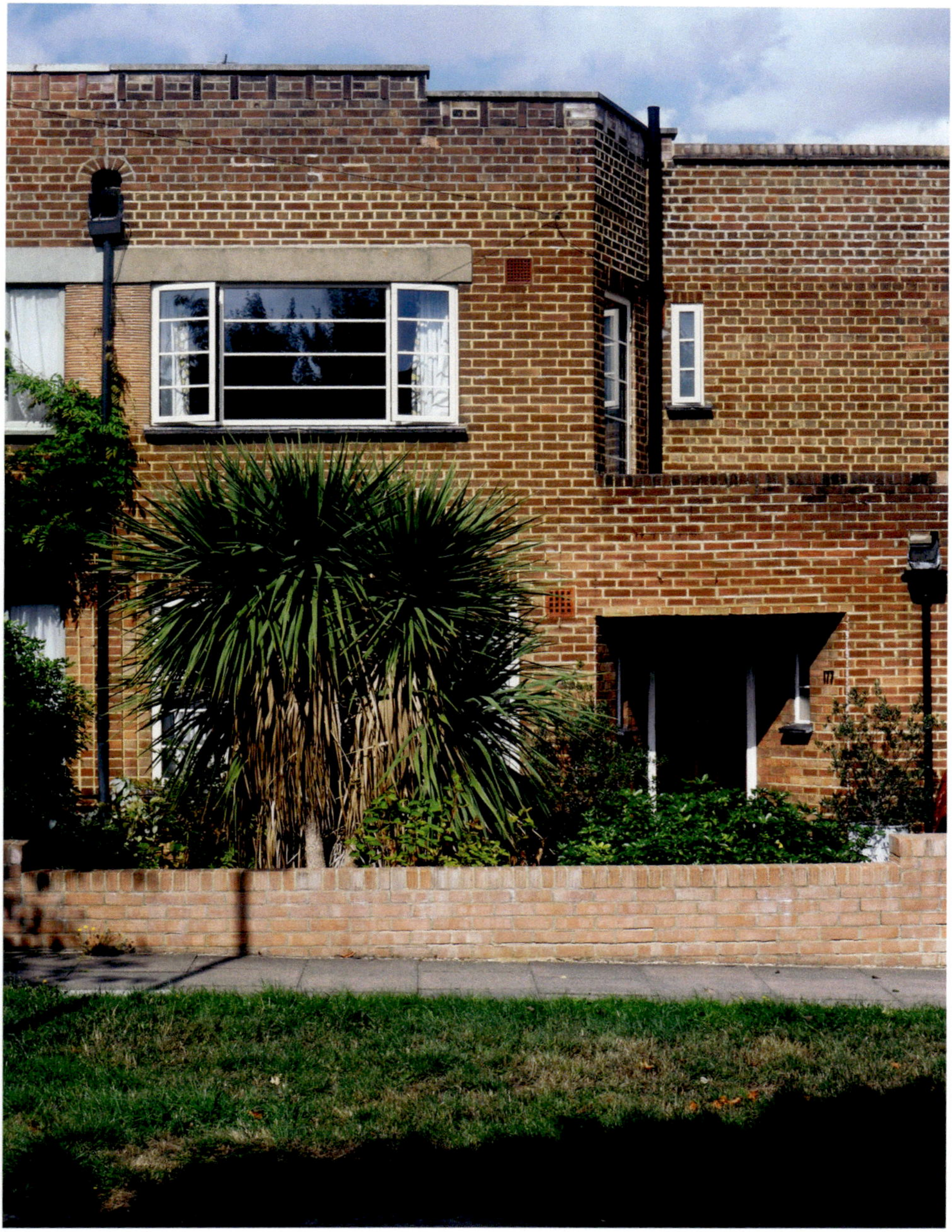

Barnfield & Meadowhill, New Malden
Kingston upon Thames
1935-8
R.A. Duncan & K. Hart
Wates & Wates

On the southside side of the A3 are another group of modernist speculative houses, less in number than their neighbours in Berrylands, but possibly more interesting design wise. They were built by the Wates building company, then known as Wates & Wates, with 20 houses featuring a mixture of designs. The more modernist of the houses feature flat roofs with sun decks, square staircase towers and geometric decoration.

The other houses on the estate are slightly more traditional in appearance with pitched roofs, curbed suntrap windows and jazzy recessed doorways. Both types of houses were designed by K. Hart with R.A. Duncan. Duncan had designed a *"House of the Future"* for the 1928 Ideal Exhibition, the first in a series that would later include an effort from Alison and Peter Smithson, and he also wrote a book with the same name alongside fellow architect S. Rowland Pierce. Duncan went into partnership with Percy and Grahame Tubbs forming Percy Tubbs Son & Duncan, designing houses in Barnet, Frinton-on-Sea and Stoke Poges.

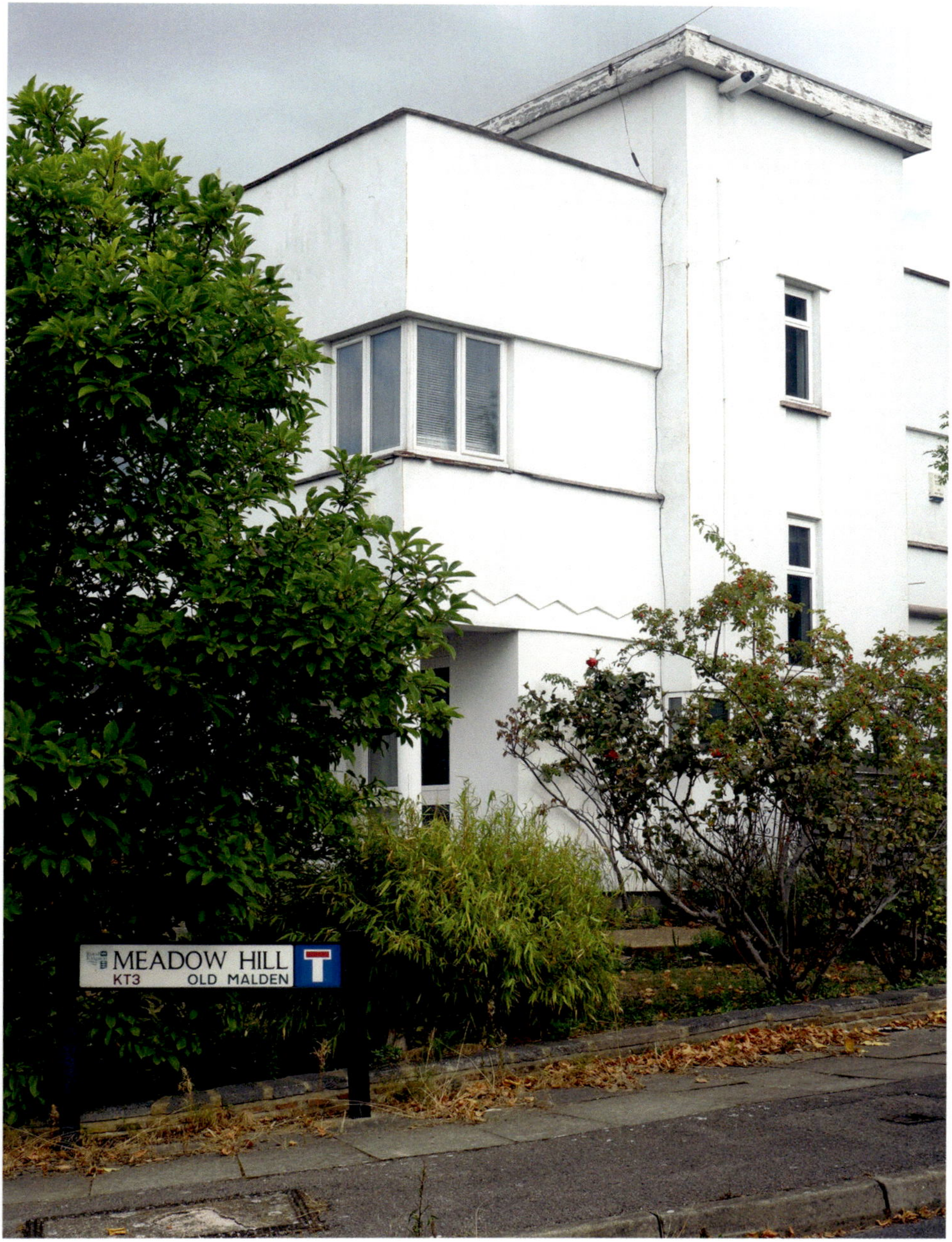
MEADOW HILL
KT3 OLD MALDEN

57, 65 & 69 Woodlands Avenue, New Malden
Kingston upon Thames
1935
Wells Coates & D Pleydell-Bouverie
E & L Berg Ltd

1-3 Wentworth Close. Long Ditton
Surrey
1934
Wells Coates & D Pleydell-Bouverie
E & L Berg Ltd

The Canadian architect Wells Coates came to fame in 1934 for his ultra-modernist design for the Isokon apartments in Belsize Park, later home to architects, designers and writers. The Isokon had been commissioned by Jack and Molly Pritchard, and Coates and David Pleydell-Bouverie then developed their Sunspan idea for the couple, exhibiting it at the 1934 Daily Mail Ideal Home Show. The house was designed to be constructed with prefabricated parts around a steel frame.

The Sunspan name came from the plan of the house, designed to be arranged on a north-south axis, admitting sunlight all day through its curved windows. Coates declined the Pritchards offer to build the houses and went with developers E & L Berg Ltd, who put up around 15 houses in the South East, including in New Malden, Long Ditton and Hinchley Wood in Surrey. Unfortunately, the builders didn't consult the architects about all of those built, making changes in plan and detail. These two groups in the south west suburbs have some alterations but are generally good examples of the Sunspan idea.

Wentworth Close, Long Ditton

Woodlands Avenue, New Malden

River Meads Avenue, Twickenham

Willow Way, Twickenham

7 The Ridings

Hanger Hill Estate, Park Royal
Ealing
1934
Welch, Cachemaille-Day & Lander
Haymills Ltd.

The Hanger Hill estate nestles just off Western Avenue, a haven of speculative modernism next to the bustle of the main road. The estate was developed by Haymills, who employed their go-to architects, Welch, Cachemaille-Day & Lander to design it. The estate is laid out with four curving crescents radiating out from Park Royal underground station and the Hotel & Garage (both also designed by Welch & Lander), with a mixture of housing styles to suit all tastes.

The Ridings contains a number of the more modernist Type 4F homes, which were three storeys high with a sun deck, 4 bedrooms and an integrated garage. There are also a number of individual designs like No.1, a large white rendered house with a curved balcony and decorative banding. Elsewhere they are designs which are more hybrid in nature, featuring pitched roofs and suntrap windows. Many of the houses have been altered, but in general the estate is probably one of the more successful interwar attempts at popular modernism.

1 The Ridings

29 The Ridings

54-60 Barn Rise, Wembley
Brent
1932
Welch, Cachemaille-Day & Lander
Haymills Ltd.

Mayfields & The Avenue, Wembley
Brent
1934
Welch, Cachemaille-Day & Lander
Haymills Ltd.

The 1924 Empire Exhibition turned Wembley from a sleepy part of Middlesex into a rapidly growing part of London. Connected to the city by the Metropolitan Railway, housing estates were built all around the town centre, looking to attract new inhabitants to 'Metro-Land'. The builders of many of these houses were Haymills Ltd, formed in Golders Green in 1911. They acquired the grounds of Wembley Golf Club in 1923, and built what became known as the Barn Hill Estate. Haymills used the firm of Welch, Cachemaille-Day and Lander to design their estates at Wembley, and later on Hendon and Ealing.

At Wembley their designs can be seen on *Barn Rise*, *Mayfields* and *The Avenue*. The Barn Rise houses are 4 semi-detached brick houses, with flat roofs decorated around the edges with tiled parapets. The houses further down the hill, on the Mayfields estate, are more obviously modernist in both intention and execution. The houses are both semi-detached and detached, with white rendered walls and sun decks. Many still survive in their original form. Also built as part of the scheme are the Lawns Court Flats, six linked low rise apartment blocks with dramatic curving entrance staircases.

Barn Rise

Mayfields

Uxendon Crescent

Boxtree Road, Harrow Weald

Clifford Way, Neasden

97-101 Park Avenue, Ruislip
Hillingdon
1933-5
Connell, Ward & Lucas
Walter Taylor Ltd

Alongside the two Lubetkin and Tecton projects featured elsewhere, these houses are probably the most ardently modernist speculative interwar houses built in London, 97-101 Park Avenue led to the "Ruislip Case" during the planning stages of these four homes. Designed by Basil Ward of Connell, Ward & Lucas for the developers Walter Taylor, the houses were to be the first of many in what was to be the "Pinnerwood Park" estate, built on land owned by King's College. The Ruislip-Northwood Urban District Council did not approve of the plans, in particular the glass staircases facing out onto the street.

After many appeals, the designs were approved with reductions in the amount of glass used and the houses were completed in 1935. Winning the court case did not help the modernist cause in the suburbs, with Walter Taylor opting not to build any more. Despite the setbacks and the tweaks, these houses are the nearest suburban speculative housing came to Le Corbusiers's *"machines for living in"*, and seems to have gained a local acceptance with a 21st century lookalike built at No.103.

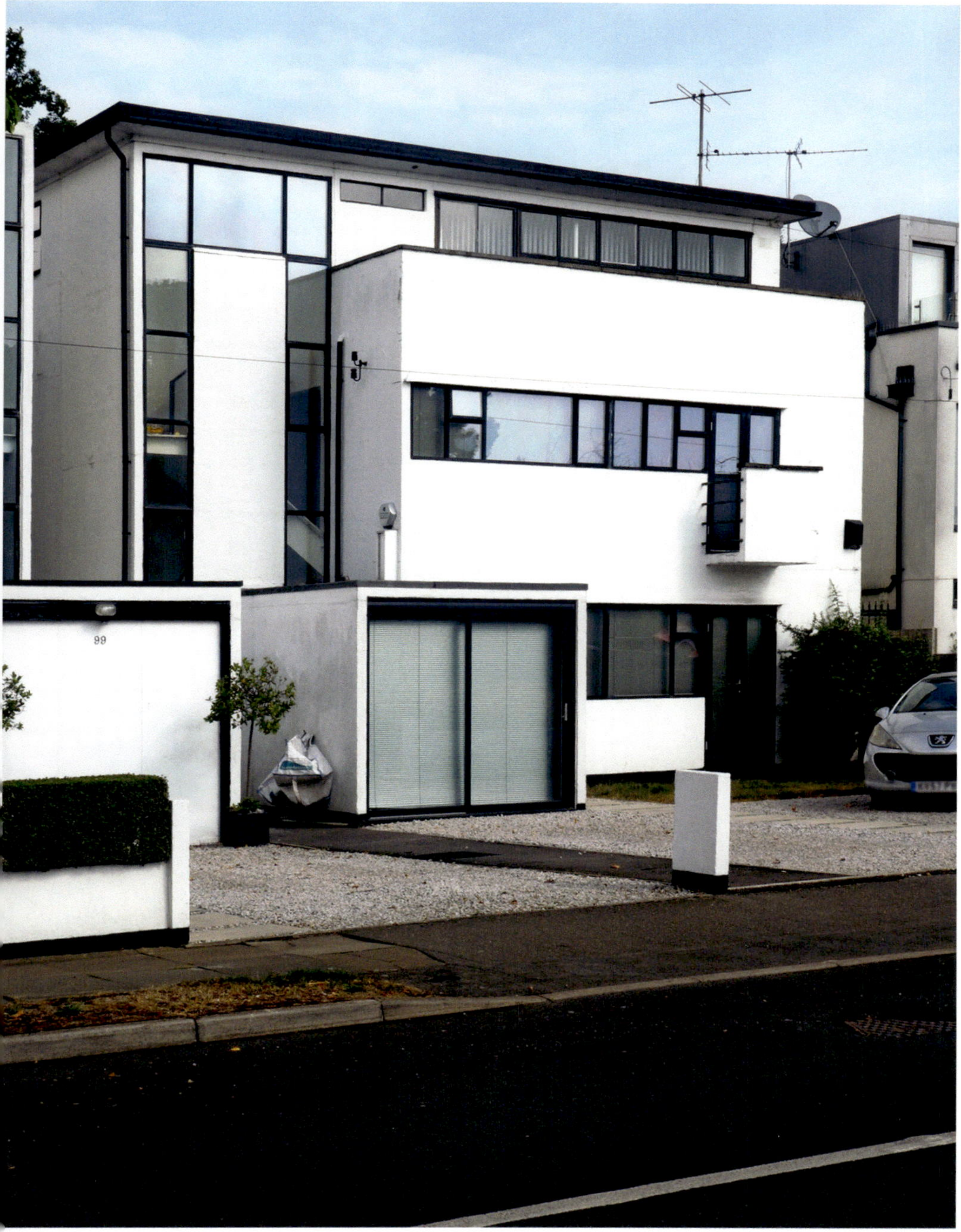
99

153-163 Northwood Way, Northwood
Hillingdon
1934
Morgan & Edwards Ltd
Morgan & Edwards Ltd

Not far from the Joel Park Estate are a group of six houses put up by builders Morgan & Edwards on Northwood Way. No architect has been identified as the designer, but the houses showcase various aspects of the interwar moderne speculative style; curved suntrap windows, white rendered walls and green pantiled parapets. A couple of the houses now have pitched roofs, but generally the group is very well kept. Their neighbours up the hill (Nos.141-151) showcase a slightly more traditional suburban style, with white walls and green tiles, but no sign of the streamlined windows or flat roofs further down.

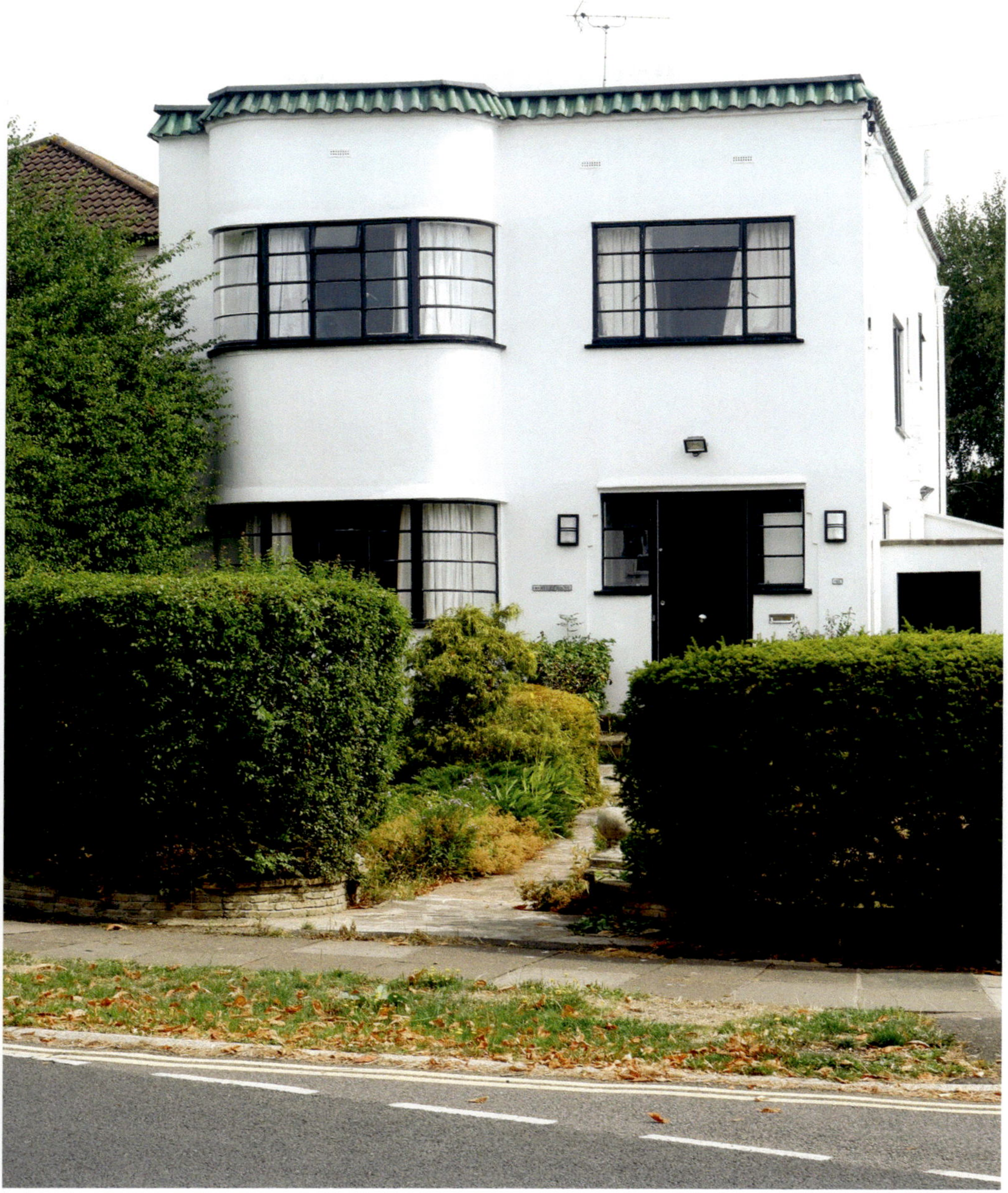

Norwich Road & Joel Street, Northwood
Hillingdon
1934
Robert de Burgh
Modern Houses Ltd

The opening of Northwood Hills underground station in 1933 (partly subsidised by developers), gave rise to a suburban development boom in this previously rural outpost of Middlesex. Architect Robert de Burgh was employed by Modern Houses Ltd to design what was known as the Joel Park Estate. Remnants of this estate can be found along Norwich Road and Joel Street, although often the flat roofs are now pitched. The semi-detached houses designed by De Burgh along Norwich Road had white rendered walls and metal windows, but strayed from the *"ornament is a crime"* dictum by including bell shaped decorations above the doorways. The houses on Joel Street are more subdued with a mixture of curved or boxy frontages and long vertical window strips.

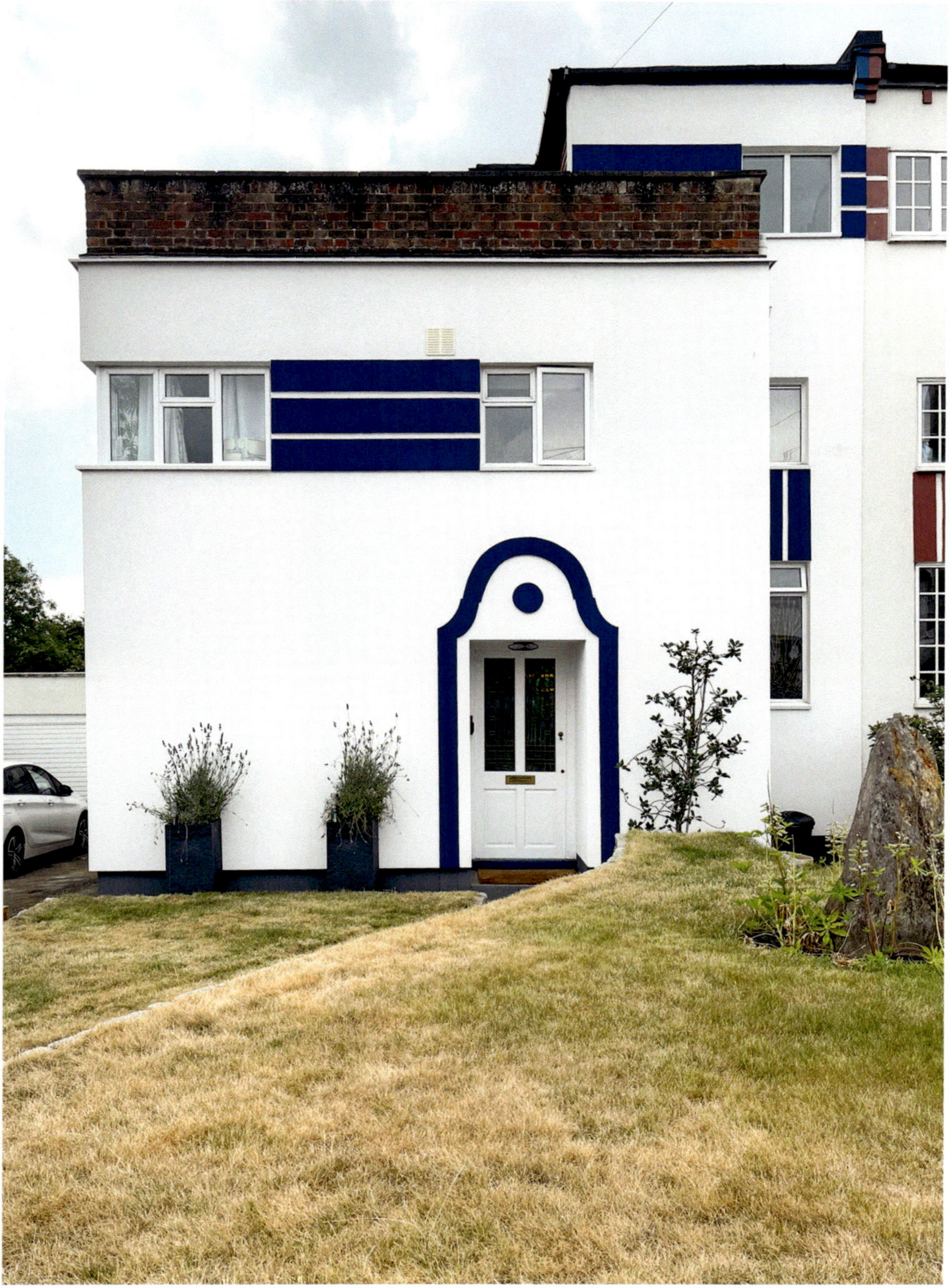

2-10 Valencia Road, Stanmore
Harrow
1935
Douglas J. Wood Architects
Warren Estate (R & E Davis)

The Warren Estate features two groups of speculative houses built on a portion of the grounds of an estate founded by the Duke of Chandos in the early 18th century. It was eventually inherited by Sir John Fitzgerald, who decided to sell parcels of land for development. Douglas Wood Architects were given the commission to build houses in 1931, but they were not completed until 1935.

The houses on Valencia Road feature an assortment of moderne features; staircase towers, metal windows and sun decks. These features, particularly the staircase towers, add to the vertical emphasis of the houses, situated as they are on a slope. Nos. 4 & 6 and 8 & 10 were built as pairs, and are largely unaltered in outward appearance. No. 2 has been extended, adding a third floor and a large Aztec-inspired door. Stanmore station, just two minutes away, had opened in 1932, allowing quick and convenient commuting to London.

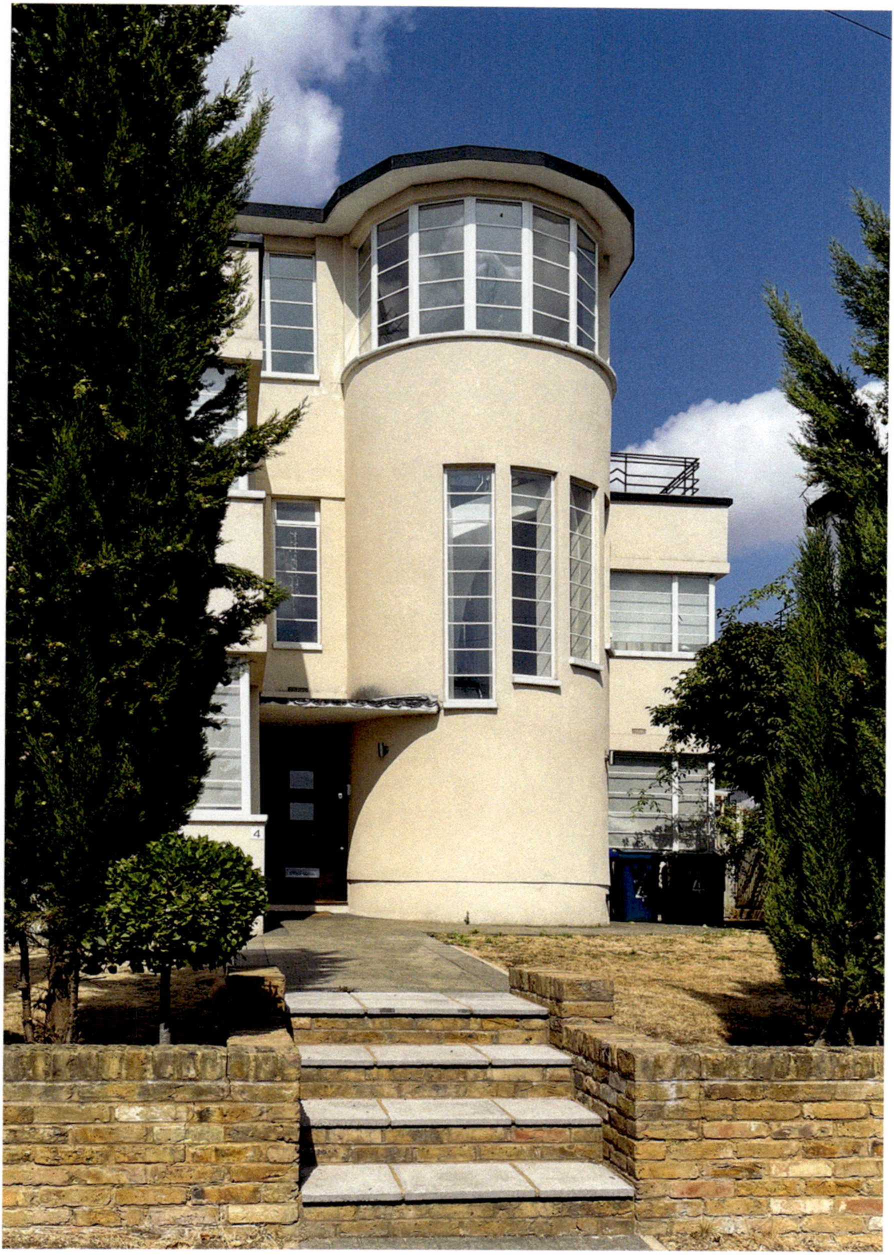

1-6 Kerry Avenue, Stanmore
Harrow
1937
Gerald Lacoste
Warren Estate (Sir John Fitzgerald)

Forming a crossroads with Valencia Road, Kerry Avenue was the second group of modernist houses built on the Warren Estate. They were designed by Gerald Lacoste, a friend of the estate owner Sir John Fitzgerald. Lacoste was only 27 at the time of the Kerry Avenue commissions and had previously been assistant to architects Edwin Lutyens and Oswald Milne, before setting up on his own and designing buildings for Gracie Fields and Norman Hartnell.

The six houses use similar features as its neighbours on Valencia Road; flat roofs, staircase towers and metal windows, but with a more horizontal emphasis. The houses are constructed of brick with a mixture of rendered and exposed brick finishes, linked to each other by their garages. A plan for a larger estate of flat roofed houses faltered, and the majority of the rest of the neighbourhood features a mixture of conventional interwar and postwar designs (aside from two commissioned houses at the top of Kerry Avenue, Nos 14 & 16). Some of the houses have been altered, with incremental additions and small extensions. Both the Valencia Road and Kerry Avenue houses are now part of a conservation area.

1 Kerry Avenue

5 Kerry Avenue

The Sun Houses. Amersham
Buckinghamshire
1933-35
Connell, Ward & Lucas
Bernard and Dorothy Ashmole

High and Over on the outskirts of Amersham was one of the first private modernist houses in Britain. Designed for Bernard and Dorothy Ashmole by Amyas Connell, it caused a sensation locally and in the architectural press. After the house's completion, the Ashmoles decided to build a modernist village on the slopes around High and Over, planning for around 30 houses. In the end only four 'Sun Houses' were built, designed by Connell and his partner Basil Ward.

The houses are built of reinforced concrete, (unlike High and Over, which was rendered brick), with gleaming white walls and metal windows. The most eye-catching part of the houses are the glazed staircases rising up to the sun decks, capped by cantilevered concrete shelters. The interiors were finished with space-saving fixtures and fittings designed by Connell and Ward. Three of the houses were sold to Charles De Peyer, a relative of Dorothy Ashmole, and one to James MacGibbon. The houses were listed in 1979, and are kept in excellent condition.

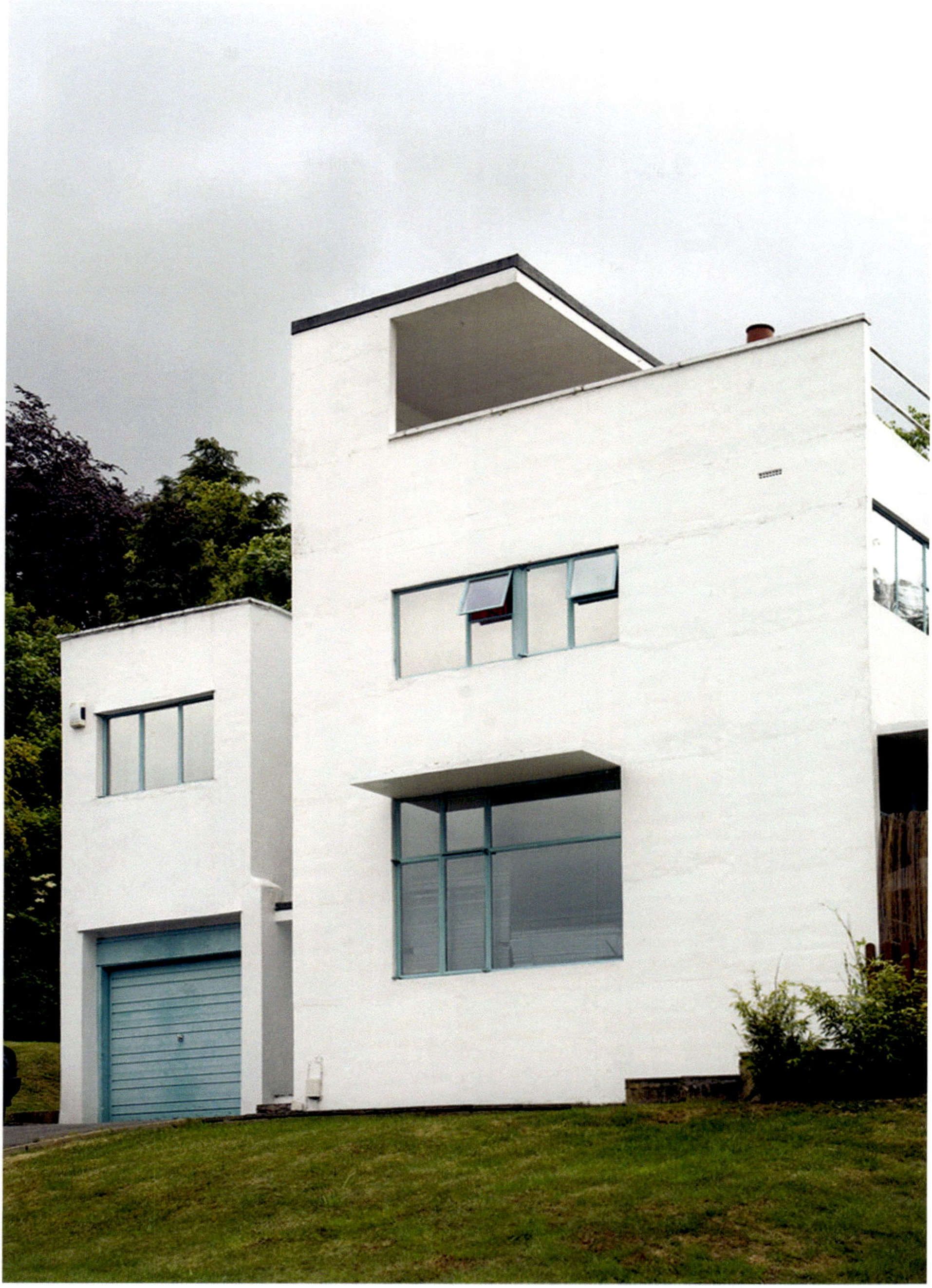